Book Prices in Renaissance Venice

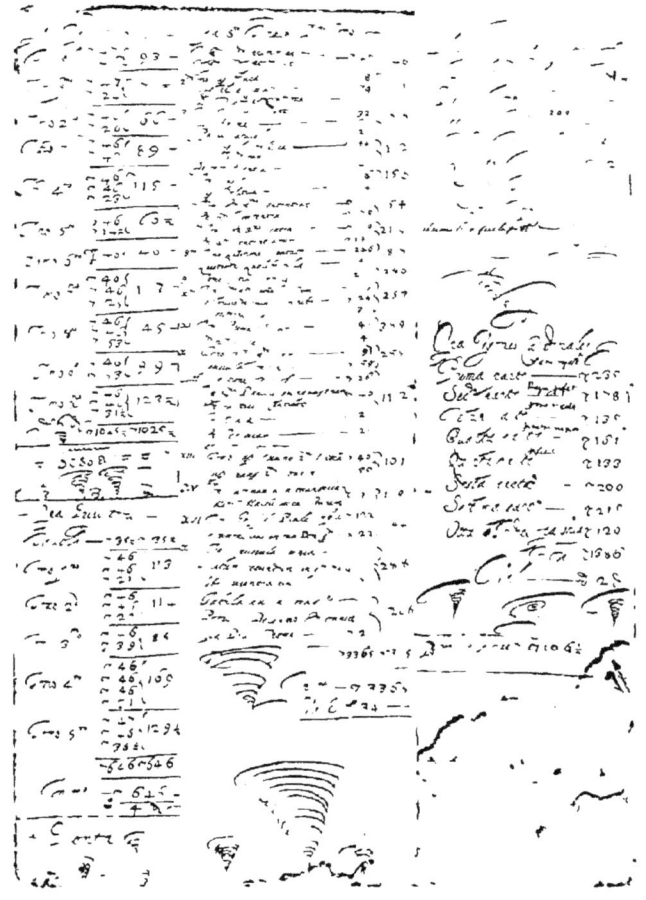

The Giunti Stockbook fol. 2v

Book Prices in Renaissance Venice: The Stockbook of Bernardo Giunti

by

MARTIN LOWRY

*Department of Special Collections
University Research Library
University of California
Los Angeles
1991*

Copyright © July 1991
by the Regents of the University of California
ISSN 1041-1143

Many fifteenth and sixteenth century presses were dynasties, but none emphasised its dependence on a heroic founder quite so much as the house of Manutius. Even in his lifetime, Aldus the Elder was regarded as irreplaceable *"squalent litterae, Aldi auxilio orbatae,"* lamented the German humanist Mutianus, when the the wars between Venice and the League of Cambrai interrupted the work of the press.[1] Contemporary publishers, whether admiring or envious, hurried to imitate Aldus' designs. The forgers of Lyons, the Giuntine press of Florence, Gerson Soncino of Fano, and the disgruntled Giovanni Bissolo of Carpi, all copied the italic type within so short a time that Aldus was compelled to seek political protection as well as legal redress.[2] The experiments of the Estienne and Colines presses with the roman type in Paris during the 1530s mark the spread of Aldus' influence after his death. His successors traded on their relationship with him by styling

---

1 *Der Briefwechsel des Mutianus Rufus* ed. C. Kraus (Cassel, 1885) Ep. 35, 42-3. On the 'dynastic" quality of many early presses, see L. Febvre and H.-J. Martin, *The Coming of the Book*, English edition translated by D. Gerrard (London Verso, 1984) pp. 144f.

2 A. F. Johnson, "Books printed at Lyons in the Sixteenth Century," *The Library*, 4th series, 3 (1922) pp. 145-174, P. Camerini, "In difesa di Lucantonio Giunta dall'accusa di contrafattore delle edizioni di Aldo Romano," *Atti e memorie della Reale Accademia di Scienze, Lettere ed Arti in Padova*, Anno CCCXCIII (1933-4) pp. 165-194, D. Fava, "L'introduzione del corsivo nella tipografia e l'opera di Benedetto Dolcibello," *Internationale Vereinigung fur Dokumentation, Dreimonatliche Berichte* IX (1942) pp. 1-7, L. Balsamo, "L'industria tipografico-editoriale nel ducato estense nel tempo di Ariosto," in *Il Rinascimento nelle corti Padane - Società e Cultura* (Bari De Donato, 1977) pp. 277-97, esp. 295-7.

themselves "*socer Aldi*" or "*Aldi filius*" in colophons: Paulus admitted to feeling the weight of his father's reputation even before he took over the responsibility for the press from his unloved Torresani cousins Buyers and collectors responded by jotting "*di Aldo*" or "*of Aldus' prynt*" beside entries in catalogues and inventories, irrespective of whether the volumes concerned had been printed in the 1490s, the 1550s or the 1580s.[3]

Though admiration for Aldus' Greek and italic types had perhaps already begun to wane when the press finally ceased production in 1597, it was gradually replaced by admiration for the liberal ideals which those types seemed to embody. The Latin italic had a special link to the literary octavo, since it was first used for a full text in the Virgil of 1501, and thereafter for a whole sequence of Latin or Italian classics Historians and bibliographers assumed that smaller books were cheaper books, and took the italic as a means of compressing the text laterally, saving paper, and so cutting costs Aldus was soon enshrined as a social liberal, bent on spreading the impact of good literature, as well as being a master of design.[4]

---

[3] N Barker, "The Aldine roman at Paris, 1530-1535," *The Library*, 5th series, 29 (1974) pp 5-20, most recently, H-J Martin, "Le Temps de Robert Estienne," in *Histoire de l'Édition Française* (3 vols, Paris Promodis, 1982-5) vol 1, pp 231-7 On the use of Aldus' name by his successors, see A Renouard, *Annales de l'Imprimerie des Aldes*, Paris 1834 ed 3, pp 73f for colophons, and 520-22, for Paulus' anxieties about maintaining the reputation of his father

[4] On timing the first use of italic see R Ridolfi, "Del carattere italico aldino nel secolo XV" *La Bibliofilia* 45 no ii (1953) pp 118-22, on cheapness, A. Johnson and S Morison, "The Chancery types of Italy and France" *The Fleuron* 3 (1924) pp 23-51 On the wider context, see L Balsamo and A Tinto, *Origini del corsivo nella tipografia Italiana del cinquecento* (Milan Il Polifilo, 1972)

It is not surprising that Aldus' successors have been overshadowed by the Titanic reputation of their founding-father, since they did much to promote it themselves. Andrea Torresani was compared unfavourably to his son-in-law and branded as a tactless profiteer by Giambattista Egnazio, even before Erasmus pilloried him in the colloquy *Opulentia Sordida*.[5] Aldus' third son Paulus has fared better as early as 1539 he was complimented on his efforts to revive the standards of scholarship associated with his father's time, and the compliment has been borne out by modern research Curt Buhler's analysis of stop-press corrections in some of the earliest Roman editions shows in Paulus the same spirit of self-criticism that had led Aldus to say that he would spend a ducat to redeem every error he had made The range and quality of the editions which Paulus printed for the *Accademia Veneziana* between 1558 and 1561 have been justly admired. But his father's reputation sat heavily on his shoulders even his private letters suggest that he measured every achievement of his own against that pitiless standard, as part of his duty to preserve "the prestige of this house." His move to Rome after the collapse of the *Accademia* in 1561, and his subsequent reliance on a papal monopoly of liturgical texts, are symptoms of the changing times and of the retreat from humanist ideals.[6] Alongside

---

[5] For a general review of the sources on Torresani, see M Lowry, *The World of Aldus Manutius* (Oxford Blackwell, 1979) pp 76-8

[6] E. Pastorello, *Inedita manuziana, 1502-1597* (Florence Olschki, 1960), no 307, pp 27f, A Johnson, "Some types used by Paolo Manuzio," *The Library*, 4th series, 19 (1938) pp 167-75, C Buhler, "Paulus Manutius and his first Roman printings," *Papers of the Bibliographical Society of America*

his father and grandfather, Paulus' son Aldus the Younger seems little more than an intellectual playboy, precociously gifted but lacking the commitment of his precessors. Even his father regarded him as being too weak to marry and follow a career, but insufficiently determined to pursue the religious vocation that might have spared his poor constitution. Unable to make a clear decision between scholarship and editorship, he ended with few solid achievements in either field, and is remembered chiefly for his efforts to redeem his fortunes by selling the family library to the pope.[7]

I found a significant indication of modern interest in the Aldine press by leafing through the index to eleven leading Anglo-American periodicals between the years 1933 and 1970. of eleven entries under the heading "Aldine press," nine related to the time of Aldus the Elder.[8] The story of the press has acquired many of the qualities of a moral tale: a visionary founder is followed by a conscientious but less imaginative son, and eventually by a spendthrift grandson who squanders the work of the previous generations. It is a kind of bibliographical

---

6 (Continued) 46 (1952) pp 209-14; P Rose, "The Accademia Veneziana science and culture in Renaissance Venice,' *Studi veneziani* 9 (1969) pp 196-242; L. Bolzoni, "L'Accademia veneziana splendore e decadenza di una utopia enciclopedica," in L Boehm and E Raimondi, *Società scientifica in Italia e in Germania dal Cinquecento al Settecento* (Bologna Il Mulino, 1981) pp 117-67

7 Renouard, *Lettere Manuziane inedite, copiate sugli autografi nella Biblioteca Ambrosiana* (Paris, 1834) p 55; P de Nolhac, *La bibliothèque de Fulvio Orsini* (Paris 1887) pp 245f; J Bignami-Odier, *La Bibliothèque Vaticane de Sixte IV à Pie XI* (Studi e testi No 272, Città del Vaticano, 1973) p 81

8 *Index to Selected Bibliographical Journals, 1933-1970* (London Bibliographical Society, 1982)

soap-opera, the saga of one family's passage "from clogs to clogs in three generations", and its very simplicity should attract our suspicion.

The aim of this paper is not to question the fundamental facts of the rise, maturity, and decline of the Aldine press, but to re-examine some of the moralising undertones which have crept into the story over the centuries. In the first place I wish to question whether the elder Aldus really held some of the attitudes attributed to him. I do not believe that Aldine books were ever intended for a mass-market, or that they were ever cheap. They were copied not because they had revealed a new audience for literary texts, but because they were beautiful, and fashionable. In the first decade of the sixteenth century Aldine texts were probably the most expensive books on the market in their various ranges. In 1600 they still held the top of the market, and controlled a remarkable proportion of it. My second theme is that Paulus and Aldus the Younger perhaps deserve rather more credit and scholarly attention for this consistency than they have received. In seeking to establish these points I shall be using some evidence that is well known and thoroughly studied, some that is known, but neglected, and some that has only recently become available.

In spite of warnings from expert typographers such as Harry Carter that using an italic fount does not necessarily save space, the notion that the octavo text set in italic was at least relatively cheap has survived much longer than it had any right to do.[9] So far as I can see, the idea rests on no contemporary

---

9 *A View of Early Typography to About 1600* (Oxford University Press, 1969) pp. 73-6

evidence and derives entirely from modern preconceptions about the paperbacked edition in what now seems a similar, small format. When he petitioned the Venetian senate for protection of his italic fount, Aldus called it only "*cancelleresca di somma bellezza, non mai più facta.*" He emphasised its beauty, not its economy. Erasmus picked up the same point when he called the letters "*minutioribus illis omnium nitidissimus.*" This is negative evidence, of course but the public advantage of the cheap book had been stressed by Gianandrea de Bussi as early as 1468, and was invoked at intervals during the 1490s by publishers who claimed to be serving the interests of the academic market.[10] The argument was available, if Aldus had wished to use it. The only direct contemporary allusion to the price of the octavos is the acid comment of Isabella d'Este, that they were not worth half of the sum asked. She was alluding to the four copies specially printed on vellum that Aldus had sent her, which were not typical, but the mere fact that vellum copies were printed suggests that the editions were aimed at the upper end of the market.[11]

---

10 Text of Aldus' appeal in C Castellani, *La stampa in Venezia dalla sua origine alla morte di Aldo Manuzio seniore* (Trieste Edizioni Lint, 1973, 2nd ed) pp 75f, Erasmus' comment in *Opus Epistolarum* (12 vols, Oxford Clarendon Press, 1906-58) vol 1, p 439, on the cheapness of printed books, see M Miglio, *Giovanni Andrea de Bussi - prefazioni alle edizioni di Sweynheym e Pannartz, protottpografi romani* (Milan Il Polifilo, 1978) p 4, allusions to the importance of cheap books to students in R Fulin, "Documenti per servire alla storia della tipografia veneziana," *Archivio veneto* 23 (1882) nos 20, 33

11 Noted by A Luzio in *Giornale storico della letteratura italiana* 6 (1885) p 276

There are good circumstantial reasons for believing that both the italic script and the smaller book may have had exclusive, rather than popular associations when Aldus launched his programme of octavos in 1501 The cursive was a development of the upright roman hand which had been the accepted style for literary texts since the second quarter of the fifteenth century: it was adopted by the younger members of the esthetic *beau monde* like Pietro Bembo, and by the fashionable scribes such as Bartolomeo di San Vito who directed their tastes [12] The small book had a very different, but equally fashionable appeal In 1474 and 1475 Nicholas Jenson had produced two tiny editions of the *Office of the Virgin* in sedecimo and trigentesimo format, printed in black and red and perhaps intended partly to perfect the technique of his press-teams with the new gothic founts which he had designed for his legal texts. Surviving copies are very rare, and most carry the crests of noble families But the potential of the small printed text for private devotion soon became evident, especially to Jenson's French successors such as Antoine Vérard Ownership of a Book of Hours had been a coveted mark of status in French society since the fourteenth century, and Goff lists ninety-six editions of the *Hours of the Virgin* and twenty-three of the *Office* before 1500 seventy-three of the first, and nineteen of the second are in octavo or smaller format.[13] If we judge the Aldine octavo as

---

12. J Wardrop, *The Script of Humanism - Some Aspects of Humanist Script 1468-1568* (Oxford University Press, 1963) B Ullman, *The Origins and Development of the Humanistic Script* (Rome Edizioni di storia e letteratura, 1960)

13 *Incunabula in American Libraries - a Third Census of Fifteenth-Century Books Recorded in North American Collections* (New York Bibliographical

an economic experiment, and neglect its double appeal to the buyer's emotions, we risk separating the book completely from its historical background But in any case the economic evidence, if rightly read, is unambiguous. Aldus' books were expensive.

The three Aldine catalogues of 1498, 1503, and 1513 have been known and studied since Renouard's time. Full-sized reproductions are available in Orlandi's edition of the Aldine prefaces, and the material available there has recently been expanded further by Klaus Wagner's notes on the prices paid by Ferdinand Columbus for his copies in the 1530s.[14] So there is no difficulty in establishing that the price of a larger octavo text like Cicero's *Epistulae ad Atticum* or Caesar's *Commentaria* was 2 lire, of the medium-sized editions such as Virgil, Horace, Statius and Martial, 1 lira 10 soldi, and of the shortest volumes like Lucan's *Pharsalia*, 1 lira only But this very precise information is so isolated that it has been possible even for a judicious critic like Harry Fletcher, who is well aware that the sums asked were more than an ordinary buyer could afford, to

---

13 (Continued) Society of America, 1972) II 338-438, O 32-55 On the appeal of the Book of Hours see Janet Backhouse, *Books of Hours* (London British Library Publications, 1985) The observations on Jenson's miniature books are based on my work for *Nicholas Jenson and the Rise of Venetian Publishing in Renaissance Europe* (Oxford Blackwell, 1991)

14 Renouard, *Annales*, pp 330-35, for printed versions of all catalogues up to 1591; P Leicht, "I prezzi delle edizioni aldine del '500," *Il Libro e la stampa*, Anno VI, iii (1912) pp 74-84, adds material from manuscript notes on a surviving copy of the 1513 list, G Orlandi, *Aldo Manuzio editore* (2 vols, Milan Il Polifilo, 1975) Plates IX, X, XI, for photographs of the originals, K Wagner, "Aldo Manuzio e i prezzi dei suoi libri," *La Bibliofilia* 77 (1975) pp 77-82

conclude that "the books did not represent the sort of staggering capital investment that the large volume of text and commentary often commanded." When a skilled workman was earning around 3 ducats – say 20 lire per month – he would have to think twice before spending ten per cent of his wages on a book but at least he could think, rather than merely yearn. In other words, Aldine literary octavos were still expensive in the absolute sense. but they were cheaper than anything that had been seen on the market until 1501 [15]

Testing this hypothesis means comparing the price of Aldus' literary octavos with that of the quarto or smaller folio editions of the same popular texts which had held the field in the 1480s and 1490s. The means of doing this are ready to hand in the register of the Venetian bookseller Francesco de Madiis, which has been well known for more than a century and is now in the Biblioteca Marciana. It pains me to say that I think a heavy responsibility for the failure to bring this key source to bear on the question of book prices rests with an English scholar. Horatio Brown was among the first to study the register after Cecchetti had discovered it. Realising its importance, he used it in his study of *The Venetian Printing Press* in 1891 to conjure up a vivid picture of the expanding market, and published parts of it as an appendix But Brown's treatment of the document has a puzzling, even slightly sinister side By asserting that the records covered only the period from May 1484 until October 1485, and that they were not extensive

---

15 "Octavo sizes and prices," in his *New Aldine Studies* (San Francisco Rosenthal, 1988) pp 88-91

enough to reveal any general trends, he seemed to imply that his very partial transcription contained all that really mattered But by referring to Fridenperger's edition of Lucretius, which does not even appear in the records until February 1487, Brown also revealed that he knew how much he omitted In fact the register lists forty-five months of continuous sales, from May 1484 until the middle of January 1488, yielding copious information about the movement of prices Brown must have realised he could not assimilate it himself but was evidently unwilling to share it with other scholars So he brushed the sand over his tracks [16]

The range of material contained in the de Madiis register is so enormous that it is impossible to extract any general conclusions without the aid of a computer I spent much of 1988 feeding more than 12,000 entries into a database, identifying as many of the editions as possible and noting their prices against the date of each sale. Fortunately, Francesco was a careful book-keeper who recorded his sales under consistent headings or titles, often identifying the printer by name and hardly ever omitting a price, unless the book concerned was part of a larger purchase for which he recorded only the total figure I shall make no attempt to present more information in this essay than bears directly on the movement of book-prices in Venice a decade before Aldus arrived on the scene.

---

[16] Biblioteca Marciana, Venezia, MS it cl XI, 45 (7439) Brown's comments can be found on pp 36-9 of his text, and his transcriptions on pp 431-52 Better use of the document is now being made by another "inglese italianizzato" – N Harris – in *Bibliografia dell' "Orlando inamorato,"* (Modena Edizioni Panini, 1988) pp 16f

First, an uneven but in some cases precipitous decline in prices had already begun. The most significant evidence is offered by the smallest, but perhaps the most important book – the little reading primer called the *Psalteriolo*, of which no printed copy now survives. It first appears at a price of 3 or 4 soldi during the entries of summer, 1484 three years later copies were being sold in batches of 30, 50, or 100 at a price equivalent to 1 soldo – an eighty percent drop which lends an element of truth to the most extravagant contemporary boasts about the cheapness of printed texts.[17]

Second and more important for our present discussion, the popular classical texts played a large part in this decline and did a good deal to bring it about The composite volumes of text and commentary which have frequently been blamed for the "high price" of books before Aldus appeared on the scene, were in fact among those whose prices show the most consistent fall. The demand for these books was such that printers competed against one another by compressing each edition into a smaller number of pages so as to economise on paper and cut the price of a copy. Sometimes we can follow the process in detail by aligning Francesco de Madiis' records with the bibliographical manuals During 1484 Francesco was probably dealing in copies of Andrea Torresani's edition of Cicero's *Epistulae ad Familiares*, which had appeared on 31 January It

---

17 De Madiis MS fo 112r (50 psalterioli sold for 2L 10s). On the text concerned see P. Lucchi, "La Santacroce, il Salterio e il Babuino libri per imparare a leggere nel primo secolo della stampa," *Quaderni storici*, Anno XIII, 2 (1978) pp 592-630 For boasts about the cheapness of printed texts see n 10, above

was a folio of 266 leaves with the commentary of Hubertinus Clericus, and sold for 3 lire unbound During the summer of 1485 the price of this very popular title fell back to 2 lire 10 soldi or even 2 lire, perhaps because Baptista de Tortis had published a shorter, 240-leaf edition And when Andreas de Paltasichis printed an even shorter, 208-leaf version on 18 June, 1487, the price dropped yet again, to 1 lira 10 soldi – exactly the sum asked by Aldus for his plain octavo text of 1512 [18]

If we compare the prices quoted in Aldus' lists of *"librorum enchiridii forma"* with those asked for the same titles by Francesco de Madiis in the 1480s, we can make the same equation in almost every case *"Virgilius cum Servio"* started in Francesco's records at 3 lire, but came down quickly to 2: the poems without the commentary could be had for 1 lira 5 soldi A plain text of Horace could also be had for 1 lira. with the commentary of Landino it cost from 1 lira 15 soldi to 2 lire. Caesar's commentaries started at 2 lire, and dropped quickly to 1 lira 10 soldi Plain texts of Sallust or Juvenal, for which Aldus charged 1 lira, could be bought from Francesco de Madiis for 10 and 15 soldi respectively In only a few cases such as Lucan or Juvenal, where the commentaries of pseudo-Ognibene, Merula or Calderini inflated the earlier texts considerably, is the price of the Aldine octavo lower than that of the folio or quarto editions available in the mid-1480s: in

---

18 E g, de Madiis MS fols 12v, 82r, 93v the most likely editions are *Gesamtkatalog der Wiegendrucke* (vols 1-, Leipzig and New York Hiersemann and Kraus, 1925-, hereafter *GW*) 6838 (Torresani), 6840 (de Tortis) and 6841 (Paltasichis)

several cases it is somewhat higher.[19]

The price of Aldine Greek texts was criticised as early as 1498 by the Bolognese humanist Codrus Urceus, who significantly fixed on the point most admired by modern bibliographers – that Aldus and his partners had "made much of a slight thing, by leaving huge areas of paper without text." But it is worth endorsing his point from Francesco de Madiis' records to prove that these Greek editions were not simply "expensive," but far more expensive page for page than the most costly texts on the bookstalls of Venice during the 1480s. The five volumes of Aristotle were quoted in the Aldine catalogues at prices ranging from 1.5 ducats for the fairly small logical texts to 3 ducats for the huge third volume of metaphysical writings. De Madiis' register proves that 1.5-2 ducats would have bought both volumes of Jenson's much prized edition of Plutarch's *Vitae* in Latin translation, while 3 ducats would have bought all four volumes of the huge edition of Nicholas of Lyra's commentary on the Bible that Johannes Herbort had printed for the company of Jenson and John of Cologne in 1481. It is not surprising that copies of Aristotle could still be bought in Venice a century after their publication.[20]

These figures suggest that our conception not only of the Aldine editorial programme, but of the whole direction of

---

19 De Madiis MS fols 94r (*Virgilius cum Servio*), 97v (*sine Servio*), 89r (*Horatius sine commento*), 95r (*cum commento Landini*), 92v (Caesar), 95r (Sallust), 73v (Juvenal)

20 De Madiis MS fol 13r ("Nicolao de Lyra con lo texto"), 53v (Plutarch) Text of Urceus' letter in L Dorez, "Alde Manuce et Ange Politien," *Revue des Bibliotheques* 6 (1896) pp 323-5

classical publication at the turn of the fifteenth and sixteenth centuries, may need radical revision. The composite editions of text and commentary which were popular in the 1480s and 1490s have been subjected to a good deal of criticism during the last twenty years, particularly from intellectual historians such as Carlo Dionisotti and Anthony Grafton. The main target of the attacks has been the scholarship. The ponderous antiquarianism of men like Perotti, Merula, Calderini and Giorgio Valla has been compared unfavourably to the light-footed philology of Poliziano, who knew how to concentrate on the truly problematic sections of a text and had the knowledge to resolve many of the problems. But in the background there is always an assumption that the price of these tomes was as ponderous as their intellectual content, and that it took the liberating genius of Aldus to release the plain text from the dead hand of an academic caste.[21]

The prices tell a quite different story. We should remember that the technique of joining text and commentary in the same volume derived from the law-schools of the thirteenth century, and had probably originated as a means of saving the students from buying two volumes instead of one. The technique had been applied to classical texts by Jenson's satellite Le Rouge during the mid-1470s, very probably with the same intention

---

21 C. Dionisotti, "Aldo Manuzio umanista," in *Umanesimo europeo e umanesimo veneziano* ed. V. Branca (Florence: Sansoni, 1963) pp. 213-43, esp. 219-24; A. Grafton, *Joseph Scaliger - a Study in the History of Classical Scholarship* (Oxford: Clarendon Press, 1983) vol. I, pp. 9-44.

of saving the student money [22] That was definitely the effect, if we can judge by the decline in the cost of the main commentaries reflected in Francesco de Madiis' records. His register seems to represent the later stages of a programme of price-cutting which had been in progress for ten years, and would perhaps continue for another five Since Aldus set his plain texts at a price of around 1 lira 10 soldi which had been common for both text and commentary more than ten years earlier, he can hardly have had any intention of cutting prices any further He must rather have seen his role as that of stopping the process of debasement, and setting standards of scholarship and elegance which would create a new fashion.

How far was he successful? And how far did his son and grandson maintain the standards which he had set, at least in the eyes of their contemporaries? The speed with which the italic type and the octavo form were copied, and the importance which French designers such as Claude Garamond soon attached to the Aldine model, provide proof that the Aldine texts had an immediate and widely felt impact. but they also suggest that Aldus' original versions were soon deluged in a flood of imitations, some of them a good deal cheaper than the original models.[23] His own appeal to the Venetian senate against the forgers of Lyons strengthens this impression, and when Paulus was invited to establish a press in Rome, it is

---

22 J Destrez, *La Pecia dans les Manuscrits Universitaires du XIIIe e XIVe Siècles* (Paris Vautrain, 1935) On Le Rouge's innovation, see V Scholderer, 'The first editions of Jacques le Rouge," *Gutenberg Jahrbuch* (1952) pp 47-50

23 P. Beaujon, "The Garamond Types," *The Fleuron* (1926) pp 131-79 See also references under n 2, above

significant that he had to send off to France for matrices which satisfied him.[24] But we now have a more precise source of documentary evidence on the later fortunes of the Aldine press In May 1983, the University of California, Los Angeles, purchased for the Ahmanson-Murphy collection an early seventeenth century manuscript containing the stock-lists of a member of the Giunti company of Florence and Venice. The fourth folio is inscribed "*Questi libro sie di mi Bernardino Giunti libraro in Venetia*" and dated "*adi primo marzo 1600*". Though he used the name *Bernardino*, I am fairly certain that the writer was *Bernardo di Bernardo* Giunti rather than his nephew *Bernardino di Filippo*, who does not appear to have been active in the book-trade until 1613. Born around 1540, Bernardo di Bernardo had moved to Venice to establish a branch of the main Florentine firm in 1570, and remained in business until 1613 as bookseller, with intervals in publishing from 1580 to 1598, and again from 1607 until his death The register therefore gives us a view of his investments during the second of these periods of consolidation between his expeditions into publishing. It is also important to remember that Bernardo's sister Lucrezia had married the younger Aldus Manutius in 1571, for this adds a strong dynastic interest to the overall economic importance of the register.[25]

---

24. *Lettere Manuziane inedite*, p 63 "ho scritto in Francia che mi dia mandato un impronto di madre delle più belle "

25 L. Camerini, *I Giunti tipografi editori di Firenze, 1571-1625 Annali inediti* (Florence Giunti Barbera, 1979) pp 17-20 (Bernardino), 37-8 (Bernardo di Bernardo), 218 (genealogical tree) Renouard, *Annales* pp 465f, 481, and F. Bartelucci, *Genealogia e discendenza dei Manuzio, tipografi, umanisti, editori del secoli XV-XVI* (Florence Olschki, 1961) on the marriage of Aldus

At first sight, the Los Angeles manuscript looks a model of careful accounting It is a full-sized folio volume, bound in stamped calf, rather than a narrow ledger in a loose vellum cover, like de Madiis' day-book; and it was evidently designed to give the staff of the Giunti shop access to their stock from as many different directions as possible and under as many different headings as they were likely to require. Slightly more than half of the book – the first 165 folios – lists titles under the general categories common in the library inventories or advertising fly-sheets of the time. About twenty leaves each are dedicated to literature, philosophy, theology, medicine, law, Greek and Hebrew, vernacular material printed in Venice, and – perhaps because the Giunti specialised in this kind of publication – books printed in black and red. Labelled vellum tags are attached to the first folio of each section to speed any search. Within each of these twenty-page categories, the books are arranged alphabetically, pages being cut in the outer margin and labelled with the appropriate letter like a modern address-book, to allow instant access to the relevant part of the inventory. Under each alphabetical heading, the various editions available are listed by size and price, from the large folios down to the diminutive sedecimos which were becoming increasingly popular. From folio 166, the specification changes from subject-matter to place of origin: there are lists of books from Florence – where the main office of the Giunti was situated – Rome, and Germany. These are followed by lists of the titles supplied by the various different publishing houses with which Bernardo did business, and the volume concludes with what appear to be two general lists of all the stock available, arranged alphabetically by author and title. The aim was clearly to provide an interlocking series of lists which would allow an enquiry to be processed as speedily as possible; and the well-thumbed edges of the pages leave little doubt that this was how the volume was used.

It may in fact have been the stock-book's very convenience that undermined this carefully planned system, and left the register bristling with the tantalising puzzles which now confront the reader. Though Bernardo inscribed his own name at the beginning of the register and implied that what followed represented a full inventory of his stock at the start of the new year and the new century, it is quite clear from the variation of the hands that made the entries that the book remained in use for a number of years. In that time Bernardo either grew rather careless and slapdash or – more probably, I think – came to rely on assistants whose understanding of the system was inferior to his own. Whether they stem from different people or from the same person in widely different moods, at least three hands seem to me to be distinguishable. The first is a small, precise italic traced with a finely trimmed pen in the style recommended by the writing manuals of the sixteenth century. Possibly this was Bernardo in his first, careful mood. At all events, the writer noted the first titles in the lists of literary and philosophical texts, and it is tempting to identify him with the sober, conscientious individual who planned the cross-referencing systems and cut the alphabets into the edges of each twenty-page category. This hand disappears after f. 47,

and is replaced by two successors which alternate throughout
the remaining pages of the volume One is a similar, orthodox
italic, written in a larger form and with a broader quill: this
script seems to me the nearest of the three to Bernardo's
proclaimed autograph on f. 4. The other writer dashed loopy,
steeply slanted letters across the page with a panache which
would become commoner as the new century developed, and
it is this hand that seems to me most likely to be that of an
assistant For compared to his methodical colleagues, this
writer reminds one of the idle apprentice in Hogarth's famous
series of prints. If he had time to spare and space to fill, he
liked to play at calligraphy: if work was pressing, he made his
entries anyhow and in any nook or cranny he could find. The
alphabetical lists at the end of the volume, both of which are
in his hand, are clearly fragmentary. the endpapers squirm with
his variegated doodles, which include a geometric flower, a bee
leaving it to fly up the page, and apparently a rough calculation
of what his salary was going to be in lire calculated at 6 4 to
the ducat. The list of vernacular titles, which contains over
2,000 entries on its twenty-seven folios, is at times illegibly
cramped and confused

Francesco de Madiis' entries of authors' names and titles
are often oblique, but at least they are consistent and can in
most cases be tracked in the array of bibliographical manuals
available for the fifteenth century. At its best, the Giuntine
stock-book records the publisher, the price, and a further piece
of information which seems sometimes to signify the number
of copies available, and at others the number of pages which

a particular edition contained. In the incomplete alphabetical lists which conclude the volume, the symbol "7" is definitely used to apply to the number of pages But in the lists of titles it cannot possibly bear the same meaning, as it repeatedly introduces numbers far lower than that of the pages in the edition concerned. This kind of inconsistency is the rule throughout. The note of price, publisher, number, or all three may be missing and when this happens with a half-understood or vaguely worded entry such as "*Grammatica Sedismo*" or "*Epitome Pantoleonis,*" the reader is left groping in helpless perplexity. Even the subtle cross-referencing system became entangled in the good intentions that had brought it into being The same title may be recorded under, say, "*Aristotelis,*" "*Ethica,*" and even "*Opera,*" and unless printer, price and numbers in stock are all recorded in every case one has little chance of telling whether one, two, or three editions are being listed In other words, we are dealing with a document which has neither the precision of the Aldine printed catalogues nor the broad view of price-movements yielded by Francesco de Madiis' continuous records.[26]

But with all its faults, the Los Angeles manuscript has qualities and associations which make it a unique source First, it reflects the state of a leading bookseller at a very sensitive moment in the history of Venetian publishing – four years after the guild had petitioned the senate for protection against

---

[26] The manuscript's call number is Collection 170/622 in the Department of Special Collections, UCLA The description and interpretations are my own, and will no doubt be much modified by future studies

privileges enjoyed by Roman printers on the ground that the number of publishers in the republic had declined from 125 to 40. Second, the register was drawn up three years after the death of the younger Aldus in Rome. By categorising his stock under certain broad headings, Bernardo Giunti enabled us to isolate the fields in which the Aldine press had been predominant. Bernardo was Aldus' brother-in-law; but he was also the representative of a family which had been among the first to copy the literary octavo in italic, and which had been taken to court by Aldus the Elder for its efforts. This ambiguous relationship between the two publishing houses had persisted. In 1561, Paulus Manutius wrote warmly to his brother of the help that Tommaso Giunti had given him in assembling types for his move to Rome, but he was well aware of rumours that Tommaso saw the scheme as a heaven-sent opportunity of getting rid of his main rival.[27] Like Francesco de Madiis' records, the Giuntine register lists editions from all the printing-houses with which it dealt alongside each other, so it is possible to see the prices of Aldine editions among the ruck of their competitors, not in the splendid isolation of their own advertisements. Finally, by comparing the prices recorded by Bernardo Giunti with those listed in the Aldine catalogues, we can see how Aldine editions had fared in the market across the whole course of the sixteenth century. Bernardo's stock-book is the last of a triad of sources which can help us to plot the movement in the price of books in Venice over the first one

---

27. Renouard, *Lettere Manuziane inedite*, pp. 62f.

hundred and twenty years of printing, and, less directly, to see how successful Aldus' followers had been in preserving his heroic reputation [28]

So far I have been able to decipher (if not always identify) the titles of 370 *libri in umanità* and 163 *libri greci e ebrei*. The second of these categories is much the easier to handle Only one Hebrew book is listed – a quarto Bible costing 3 lire 10 soldi, which was probably the version printed by Giovanni di Gara in 1595 The relatively small number of editions and the clear naming of authors make most of the Greek texts identifiable, and duplicated entries can usually be detected. The *libri in umanità* are a much less tractable selection, partly because the category was not so clearly defined They include a broad selection of classical Latin and humanist literature, with Cicero, whether in the original or in translation, remaining the most popular single author. But there are also a good many philosophical or scientific works such as the *Logica* of Paulus Venetus or Latin translations of Aristotle, there is an immense range of grammars and dictionaries, many of which I have been quite unable to identify, and a number of recognisable but erroneous entries like the *libro di Polifilo in Latino* (sic) which do nothing to reinforce confidence in the accuracy of the others

---

28 Brown, *The Venetian Printing Press*, pp 89f for doubts on the interpretation of the petition, see P Grendler, *The Roman Inquisition and the Venetian Press, 1540-1605* (Princeton, 1977) pp 225-9 On the alleged plagiarism of Lucantonio Giunti, see the article of Camerini cited under n 2

But the lasting influence of the Aldine press is obvious throughout. Of the 370 entries under *libri in umanità*, fifty-seven are identified as "*di Aldo*" in the manuscript, and another fifteen, though undeclared, are most easily traced to the same press Two editions – the poems of Augurello and Lucan's *Pharsalia*, seem to date from the time of Aldus the Elder. Twenty-two come from Paulus' time, and the remaining thirty-three from the age of Aldus the Younger Though all the other great publishing houses of the time are named in the lists – Griffo, Scoto, Valgrisi, Marcolini, Giunti, Giolito – none is represented by more than twenty titles.[29]

Among the Greek and Hebrew editions the proportions are much the same. Of the 163 entries listed, thirty-four are named as Aldines, the nearest rival in this case being the Giuntine press of Florence Its fifteen editions are identified by the phrase "*da Fiorenza.*" But the Greek catalogue as a whole shows a different pattern from its Latin counterpart As we saw and as we would expect, the greater part of the *libri in umanità* had been published at a relatively recent date, thirty-three of the Aldines coming from the time of Aldus the Younger and only two or three dating back to the time of his grandfather. With the Greek texts this proportion is almost exactly reversed. Only one was printed by Aldus the Younger, and only seven by his father Paulus fourteen of the remaining twenty-six were published by Aldus the Elder before 1515, the

---

29 The manuscript is unpaginated "*Libri in umanità*" are the first entry, covering fols 5v-24v "*Libri greci e ebrei*" are listed from 113r-122r Both categories are much less full than Law, Theology and Italian literature

other twelve by his Torresani successors before 1540 The Giuntine texts show exactly the same pattern: eight of the fifteen listed were printed before 1530 It is difficult to say whether this decline in the importance of Greek publishing during the central quarters of the century reflects the growing influence of the inquisition, the loss of the restricted market to French or Flemish printers such as Estienne and Plantin, or a conscious change of direction by the Italian publishers. Probably it was a combination of all three But I think the isolated Hebrew Bible offers an interesting piece of indirect evidence. Permitted in an expurgated form by Sixtus V for circulation among Jewish communities, it was available and advertised on the list. It has no Greek counterpart The only biblical texts available in Greek are psalters, one in octavo, the other sedecimo Whether we blame the inquisitors or economic forces, religious publishing had changed since Aldus, Froben, and Cardinal Ximenes' team in Alcalà had competed to put the Greek text of the Bible into print for the first time.[30]

The mere number of Aldine editions advertised in the Giunti catalogue does not necessarily mean that the books were in demand. Three years after the death of the younger Aldus, and against the background of his debts, it could well mean that the market was choked with "remainders" which

---

30 On the issues involved and the edition see D Amram, *The Makers of Hebrew Books in Italy* (London Holland Press, 1963) pp 358-63, Grendler, *The Inquisition* pp 254f, Lowry, *Aldus Manutius* pp 286f, B Hall in *Cambridge History of the Bible* (3 vols., Cambridge University Press, 1963-70) vol 1 pp 39-93, J Bentley, *Humanists and Holy Writ New Testament Scholarship in the Renaissance* (Princeton 1983) pp 70f

Bernardo had used his family connection to acquire in large numbers to sell at a discount. This is what we would expect, and it would be consistent with the interpretation that Professor Rudolph Hirsch placed upon the Aldine sales-catalogues of 1586, 1589, and 1591. Pointing to the number of books on the first list which were still available on the last, and to the fact that the price of some editions – the *Epistulae* of Paulus Manutius, for example – was beginning to fall, he concluded that the press was in financial difficulty by the time Aldus went to Rome in 1587.[31] That may be the truth in general terms Paulus had been seriously concerned about his son's financial prospects as early as 1561, and had moved to Rome partly to obtain some kind of a sinecure for him. But Bernardo Giunti's register counts very strongly against any notion of a drop in the demand for Aldine texts, and against attaching any significance whatever to the mention of copies unsold after only five years. First, it makes it clear that there was nothing unusual about a book's remaining on a publisher's list for far longer than we would believe possible Many Greek authors from both the Giuntine and Aldine presses remained on the market for more than a century after their first appearance, and Bernardo advertised copies of Hermolao Barbaro's *Castigationes Plinianae*, of which I can trace no edition later than 1495.[32] Second, the pricing of the Aldine editions in comparison to their immediate competitors, that is, the same titles in the same

---

31 "The Art of Selling Books Notes on Three Aldine Catalogues, 1586-92," *Studies in Bibliography* 1 (1949) pp 83-101

32 H*2423 (Cremona, 1495)

format as produced by other publishers, makes it quite clear that there was no question of "discounting" or "remaindering." In almost every case the Aldine was the most costly edition in its class. At 12 lire or nearly 2 ducats, the Aldine was by far the most expensive of seven available editions of Ambrosius Calepinus' popular Dictionary. The nearest was priced at 7 lire, and the work was advertised as low as 1 lira 10 soldi. The folio edition of Cicero's *De Officiis* printed by Aldus the Younger in 1581 cost 4 lire 10 soldi, Bonelli's version in the same format cost 3. Sallust's histories could be had for 1 lira in the Aldine octavo. Griffo's version cost 15 soldi.[33]

With the Greek editions the pattern is exactly the same. The Giuntine text of Pollux's *Vocabularium*, published in 1520, was for some reason 3 lire more expensive than the Aldine, at 12 lire rather than 9. But the Florentine Philostratus cost only 1 lira 4 soldi against Aldus' 4 lire; an Aldine Homer cost 6 lire, while Giovanni Gatta's version could be had for 3 and Alvise Zio's for 2.[34] The successful Greek grammars of Theodorus Gaza and Fra Urbano Valeriani had first been issued in folio format by Aldus the Elder, and reduced to octavos by Paulus in 1549 and 1557. Both were priced at 2 lire in octavo. Giuntine texts of both grammars were available at 1 lira 10 soldi, and

---

[33] The most recent Aldine of Calepinus was Renouard, *Annales* p 348 (1592, no 5). For *De Officiis* see p 329 (1581, no 7) and Sallust, p 340 (1588, no 3). There had been numerous earlier editions of all three texts.

[34] Renouard, *Annales* pp 32f (1502, no 1), Camerini, vol 1 p 142 (Pollux); Renouard, *Annales* pp 26f (1501, no 2), Camerini vol 1 no 105 (Philostratus, though not the same text); Renouard, *Annales* pp 46f (Homer, 1504, no 5).

Giovanni Gatta provided Gaza's for as little as 1 lira 4 soldi In relation to their contemporaries, the editions of the Aldine were cheaper at the end of the sixteenth century than they had been at its outset.[35]

I have not subjected the Italian titles to such detailed scrutiny, partly because the Aldine press never aspired to the same dominance in this field, partly because the entries in the register are so numerous and so slapdash that there is little chance of establishing an overall view of who printed what. But particular items suggest that the broad strategy adopted by Aldus in the first decade of the century, and the reputation it had won for him, had been maintained Whether he coveted such a role or not, Aldus came to be seen as a kind of pathfinder, who published experimental works in the vernacular and sought by applying the same critical methods to the text, to associate more modern classics with the prestige that hovered over the ancients He defended the autograph manuscript of Petrarch that Carlo Bembo had provided for him as loudly as he sang the praises of the Paris manuscript of Pliny's Letters which enabled him to add a lost book to the collection. He set the price of his Italian literary texts in octavo at the same level of 1 lira 10 soldi, and made arrangements for the same special copies to be printed for

---

[35] Renouard, *Annales* p 144 (Gaza, with Chrysoloras and Guarino 1549, no 3), p 171 (Valeriani 1557, no 6) All references to UCLA MS, fol 115v

clients who required them.[36] Very much the same attitudes towards Italian are reflected in the Aldine entries in the stockbook. The old stalwarts are still on the list the *Letters* of Pietro Bembo – mentor of Aldus the Elder on the Italian language – were available for the sum of 3 lire 10 soldi. The copy now in the Ahmanson-Murphy collection binds the four small octavos as two larger ones, and suggests that the price of about 1 lira 10 soldi for a volume of moderate size had been maintained.[37] There are substantial new works, such as the *Nuova disciplina e vera arte militare* of Brancatio, in which a professional soldier fused his reading of Caesar with his forty years of campaigning in recommending that massed pike-phalanxes be replaced by smaller but intensely drilled companies of arquebusiers He wrote the work, which is an interesting pointer towards the drill-manuals of Maurice of Nassau and Gustavus Adolphus, around 1578 Aldus published it in 1585 as a 200-page folio which sold for the very high price of 4 lire.[38] A century earlier, one could have bought a full Italian text of the Bible for that sum

These figures – between 1 lira 10 soldi and 2 lire for an octavo text of average size, up to 4 lire for a smaller folio, – have a familiar ring, and they bring us at last to the most

---

36 Orlandi, *Aldo Manuzio editore* vol 1 pp 52-5, 147-51 (Nos XXX, LXXXVII, Petrarch), 94-7 (LXIV, Pliny) For comment, see C Dionisotti, *Gli umanisti e il volgare tra Quattrocento e Cinquecento* (Florence Le Monnier, 1968)

37 Ms fol 152r, UCLA Special Collections Z 233 A4 B42d

38 Ms fol 139r, UCLA Special Collections Z 233 A4B73, W McNeill, *The Pursuit of Power Technology, Armed Force and Society since 1000 A D* (Oxford Blackwell, 1982), esp pp 117-43

significant point to emerge from Bernardo Giunti's records. The price of Aldine editions had remained generally stable for almost a century. Some popular Latin texts could be had for a little less than they had cost in the second decade, a plain text of Virgil in octavo cost only 1 lira 4 soldi in 1600, and a three volume set of Ovid was down from 4 lire 10 soldi to 3 lire 12 soldi. And there were a number of offers which, through the change in bibliographical tastes, we would now regard as bargains even in their own time. The Greek grammar of Nicolaus Clenardus, a substantial octavo volume of more than 500 pages, and with a good deal of complex tabular material in two languages, could be bought for only 16 soldi. Even more striking is the case of Paetus' work on ancient weights and measures, a very beautiful folio published by Paulus in 1573 with special typeforms and illustrations of antique vessels or plough-teams at work. This could be had for only 1 lira 10 soldi.[39] But examples like these only serve to emphasise the power of demand, and the fact that demand for other Aldine texts was as strong as ever, or stronger. The younger Aldus charged 3 lire for a copy of Caesar that could have been bought from his grandfather for 2, having expanded the illustration and explanation that Fra Giocondo had included in the earliest version. If the folio Aristophanes of 1498 had declined slightly, from 18 lire down to 12 or about 2 ducats, then Pollux's *Vocabularum* had risen from 1 ducat to 1.5, and the great volumes of Aristotle were still priced at the 2 ducats each which

---

39 Renouard, *Annales* pp. 208, 216f (1570, no. 1, 1573, no. 11), UCLA Z 233 A4C59, *Z 233 A4P13

had been asked in the first catalogue Even the esoteric *Polifilo*, which had cost 1 ducat when its financial backer Leonardo Crasso appealed to the senate in 1509 for an extension to his monopoly because he had been unable to dispose of most of the copies, was still being sold at 6 lire in 1600.[40] The sixteenth century was of course a time of rapid inflation, so the mere fact that the price of books remained relatively stable means that in real terms they were a good deal cheaper. But even allowing for this, there is a complete contrast between the tumbling prices recorded by Francesco de Madiis in the 1480s, and the steady level which reaches from Aldus' advertisements at the beginning of the new century to Bernardo Giunti's stock-book at its end.

If Bernardo's records reveal that the economic value of Aldine publications had been maintained, individual copies of the editions which he offered for sale confirm that their importance and value to their readers had not declined either. Nicolas Barker has insisted in his introduction to the catalogue of the Ahmanson-Murphy collection that one of its chief fascinations lies in the number of volumes whose passage from one owner to another can be traced across the centuries from marginal notes, inscriptions, or the special quality of their

---

40 M Casella and G Pozzi, *Francesco Colonna, biografia e opere* (2 vols, Padua Antenori, 1959), vol 1 p 97 UCLA MS fol 15r This is probably the second edition, 1545, no 14 (Renouard, *Annales* vol 1 pp 133f) However, it should be noted that the MS describes the work as being in Latin, and that the title of the first edition had indeed been printed in Latin

bindings.[41] I can only reinforce his view by adding that, without taking account of the pride in possession that these marks often display, we risk misunderstanding the whole nature of the Aldine achievement. Early in the essay I suggested that Aldus designed his texts, particularly his octavos, to make them look attractive rather than to make them cost less. It remains to prove this point in detail.

Often, however, the notes suggest no particular pride or indeed any other emotion, but the sober, continuous use of professional scholars like Aldus himself Calepinus' Latin Dictionary, as we have seen, was a very expensive volume in its folio format. The library has a copy still in its original loose vellum binding, but with no other striking qualities except the careful inscriptions of five successive Florentine owners, the first in a cursive hand of the later sixteenth century, the last dated 1835.[42] Four of the five volumes of Aristotle bear the notes of a Bolognese family named Mauritius who appear, from the crisp dialectical comments in Greek and Latin on endpapers and in the margins, to have been academics. The father, Christophorus, seems to have acquired the set around the middle of the sixteenth century, his son Paulus dated his last notes in 1597, just three years before Bernardo Giunti listed similar volumes in his inventory of Greek texts As a scholarly resource for Paulus, and as an investment for Bernardo, the edition of Aristotle had retained its value.[43]

---

41. *A Catalogue of the Ahmanson-Murphy Aldine Collection at UCLA*, Fascicule 1 (Los Angeles 1989) pp xiv-xx

42 UCLA Special Collections *Z 233 A4C128 1576

43 *Catalogue*, nos 4, 11, 13, 21

In complete contrast, other books seem to have generated intense feelings rather than intellectual endeavour. Two copies of Aldus' own Latin Grammar have a certain poignancy in this respect. The first is a quite unprepossessing little volume in the octavo format of 1561, still in its contemporary binding and with loose thongs, rather than the more expensive clasps, to keep it shut For such as this Bernardo Giunti would probably have been quite content with the 1 lira 2 soldi which was its stated price. But on the titlepage is inscribed the date "*1565 die 26 Augusti*," and a note that the book had been a gift of Wolfgang Kloezd to Caspar Schmidt, as a memento of the studies they had shared in Verona. Wolfgang added his inscription below his friend's. There is no sign that Caspar used the book to advance his studies much further; in fact he may not have lived to pursue them, for the final endpaper carries the name of another owner named Seidmann and the date 1566. But the cheap little book had been a symbol of the "*Italienische Reise*" which was so vital a part of the intellectual experience of generations of German scholars A copy of the 1568 edition of the same title had an even more potent effect on its seventeenth century owner, who scrawled blood-curdling threats of emasculation against anyone who stole the book from its "boss" – *il padrone* – on the final leaf Then, perhaps a little ashamed of himself, he mildly added "Francesco Molducci erravisse sentio" – "I am conscious of my sins" – at the bottom of the page [44]

---

[44] UCLA Special Collections Z 233 A4M22cl (1561), Z 233 A4M322c (1568)

On a more serious level, some books have clearly played a part in the great cultural and political upheavals of the time, irrespective of any personal feelings or even scholarly use by their owners. Two of the Greek texts described in the first volume of the *Catalogue* are of especial importance in this respect. The Dioscurides of 1499 bears the marks of five different owners including the great Aldine expert Antoine-Augustin Renouard, who was certain that the extensive sixteenth-century notes were those of Scipio Fortiguerra, close friend of Aldus and a signatory of the famous "Statute of the Academy." I am unable to confirm or refute this judgement.[45] But the interests of the first owner are quite clear, for the margins are peppered with cross references to the *Naturalis Historia* of Pliny the Elder. This work enjoyed a brief, intense vogue during the last quarter of the fifteenth century, before detailed criticism revealed its confusion and superficiality in the meantime humanist attention to the vast range of subjects which Pliny had covered extended the influence of its philological methods into fields such as medicine and geography, besides expanding the information available about ancient art.[46] This

---

45 On Fortiguerra's role in the Academy, see my *Aldus Manutius* pp 195-202

46 A Castiglioni, "The School of Ferrara and the controversy on Pliny," in *Science, Medicine and History Essays on the Evolution of Scientific Thought Written in Honour of Charles Singer*, ed E Underwood (2 vols, Oxford University Press, 1953) vol 1 pp 269-79, and C Nauert, "Humanists, scientists and Pliny changing approaches to a classical author," *American Historical Review* 84 (1979) 72-85, Lilian Armstrong, "The Illustration of Pliny's *Historia Naturalis* in Venetian manuscripts and early printed books," in *Manuscripts in the Fifty Years after the Invention of Printing*, ed J Trapp (London Warburg Institute, 1983) pp 97-105.

Dioscurides bears the traces of its contribution to the process. In the same way, though the copy bears no marks of detailed critical use, the volume of Greek letters published in 1499 is inscribed "Episcopus attine" on the titlepage. This reference is evidently to the Basle family whose founder, Nicholas Episcopius the Elder, had married the daughter of Froben, worked alongside his successor, Herwagen, and so become heir to that great publishing-house At no stage does this press appear to have reissued the *Epistolographi Graeci*, though it was one of the pioneers of Greek typography north of the Alps. but even without evidence that it supplied its owners with copy the book is a powerful symbol of the "migration of letters" which undermined the early dominance of the Italian publishers in Greek [47] The very existence of this copy does something to explain why such a large proportion of Bernardo Giunti's Greek stock consisted of books published in the first part of the sixteenth century

Most striking of all is one of three copies of the first folio edition of the *Canones et Decreta* of the Council of Trent which Paulus published in 1564, after his move to Rome three years earlier. On the titlepage a contemporary hand has written "Prima Editio cum emendationibus MSS. et authenticis subscriptionibus Secretarii ac Notariorum Sacri Concilii " "First edition, with the manuscripts corrections and authentic signa-

---

[47] *Catalogue*, No 24 See P Bietenholz, *Basle and France in the Sixteenth Century – The Basle Humanists and Printers in their Contracts with Francophone culture*, Travaux d'Humanisme et Renaissance XCII (Geneva Droz, 1971) pp 45, 80f, 114f, C W Heckethorn, *The Printers of Basle in the XV and XVI Centuries Their Biographies, Printed Books and Devices* (London, 1897) pp 118-28

tures of the secretaries and notaries of the Holy Council." Such corrections as there are seem rather to be suggestions, since they are infrequent, do not alter the sense, and do not appear to have been incorporated in subsequent versions. But on the last blank leaf Angelus Massarellus, Marcus Antonius Peregrinus, and Cynthius Pamphilus attest that they have collated this version with the notes taken during the sessions and find it to be accurate. When set alongside the Department of Special Collections' newly acquired draft of the contract under which Paulus Manutius moved to Rome in 1561, this volume provides overwhelming confirmation of the reputation which his press still enjoyed, of its importance to the counter-offensive which the Catholic Church was about to launch, and of the survival of the high critical standards which his father had set in the first decade of the century.[48]

When aligned with the economic evidence offered by the Giunti stock-book, volumes like these must lead us to a judgement of the entire Aldine enterprise which discards any notion of cost-cutting or popularisation There is no contemporary evidence to suggest that Aldine texts were cheap, or that they were ever intended to be Aldus set the price of his smaller texts round about the level that had been established for the same titles in a larger format ten years or so earlier But by giving them a fashionable and rather exclusive look he

---

48 UCLA Z 233 A4C83 (1564) cop 3 Renouard, *Annales* pp 190-94 (1564, no 4) The importance of Massarellus' records as a source for the Council is noted by H Jedin, *History of the Council of Trent*, English edition (2 vols, London Nelson, 1957), pp 573f

raised the status of an object that had already become relatively cheap, and so raised the expectations that a buyer would have of a printed book. The large number of dedications, and the preparation of special copies on vellum, were certainly calculated to enhance the effect. Among the forty-eight patrons named by Aldus the Elder we find five highly placed clerics, including Pope Leo X, five members of Italian princely families, eight Venetian nobles of varying age and status, and a wide assortment of public servants and teachers from several different European countries. These figures take no account of authors, collaborators, or editors who often received a grateful mention in the dedications. The cumulative effect of this strategy was to make buying an Aldine text rather like joining an exclusive intellectual club, or accepting an invitation to enter the "library without walls" of which Erasmus wrote in his *Adagia*.[49] The Giunti stock-book suggests that Paulus and Aldus the Younger succeeded in maintaining a great part both of the commercial value and of the mystique with which their founding father had endowed his books. Individual volumes in the Ahmanson-Murphy collection show that the books never lost their quality to fascinate; and the very existence of that collection proves that they have not lost it yet

---

49 Figures based on Orlandi, *Aldo Manuzio editore*. The most convenient version of Erasmus' famous comment is still Margaret Mann Phillip's *The "Adages" of Erasmus a Study with Translations* (Cambridge, 1964)

I The Giunti Stockbook fol 19r: leaf including the
Hypnerotomachia Polifili

11 The Giunti Stockbook fol. 113r: leaf including
  "Catalogo de libri Greci é Ebrei".

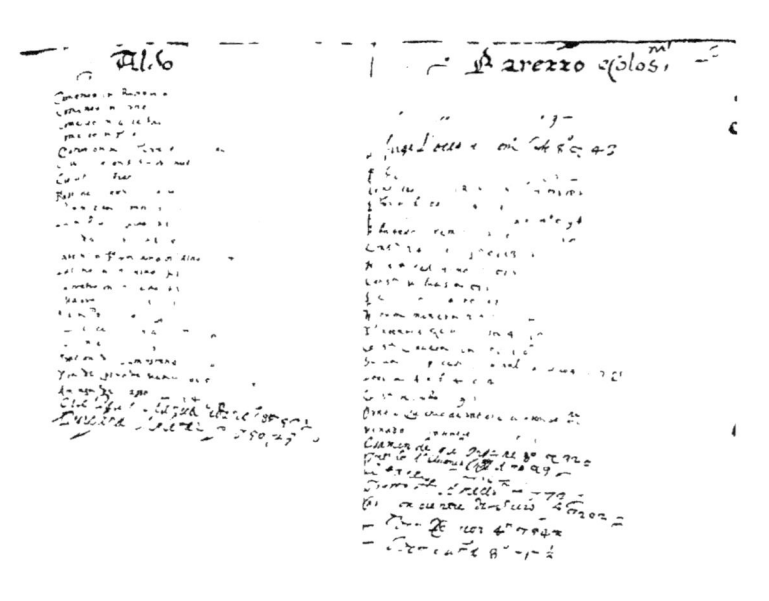

III. The Giunti Stockbook fol. 249r·
leaf including works by "Aldo".

CPSIA information can be obtained
at www.ICGtesting.com
Printed in the USA
LVHW080858161222
735312LV00004B/180